NEW BIG FUN

2

WORKBOOK

Mario Herrera

Barbara Hojel

New Big Fun
Workbook 2 with Audio CD
Pearson Education Limited

KAO Two, KAO Park, Hockham Way, Harlow, CM17 9SR, England and Associated Companies throughout the world.
www.English.com
© Pearson Education Limited 2018

Authorized Adaptation from the U.S. edition, entitled Big Fun, 1st Edition, by Mario Herrera and Barbara Hojel, published by
Pearson Education Inc, © 2014 by Pearson Education, Inc.
The right of Mario Herrera and Barbara Hojel to be identified as authors of this Work has been asserted by them in accordance
with the Copyright, Designs and Patents Act 1988.

First published 2018
Twelfth impression 2024

ISBN: 978-1-2922-6574-2

Set in Gill Sans Infant Std, Avenir LT Pro, ITC Avant Garde Gothic Std, Banco ITC Font

Printed in Slovakia by Neografia

Text composition: Isabel Arnaud
Illustration credits: A Corazón Abierto, Francisco Morales, Luis Alberto Montiel Villegas, Javier Montiel

PEARSON ELT ON THE WEB

PearsonELT.com offers a wide range of classroom
resources and professional development materials.
Access course-specific websites, product
information, and Pearson offices around the world.

Visit us at **www.pearsonELT.com**.

CONTENTS

NEW **BIG** FUN

Song

Chorus

From the sky to the ground
And all the way around—
We can have big fun!
If there's rain, if there's sun,
Let's play with everyone.
We can have big, big fun!

Take a walk outside.
Our world is big and wide.
There are flowers and trees
And yellow bumblebees.
Buzz, buzz, buzz!

(Chorus)

Join your hands with me.
Let's see what we can see!
Then take a closer look.
We'll learn beyond our book.
Look, oh, look!

(Chorus)

1 MY SCHOOL

Find and circle.

Trace and color.

Vocabulary Practice: *shelves, book, scissors, marker*
Language Practice: *These are (scissors). This is (a book).*

Look and match.

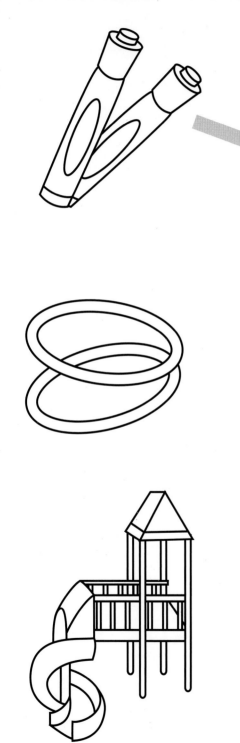

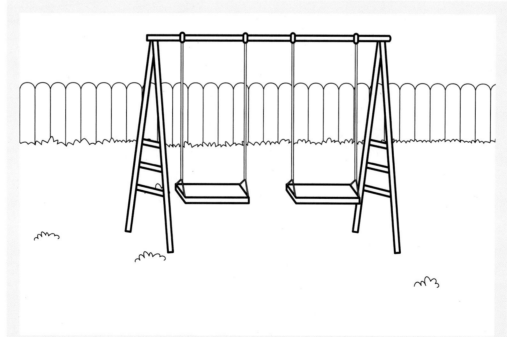

Vocabulary Practice: *inside, outside; markers, hoops, jungle gym, scissors, ball, box, books*

Look and draw a ball in each scene. Color.

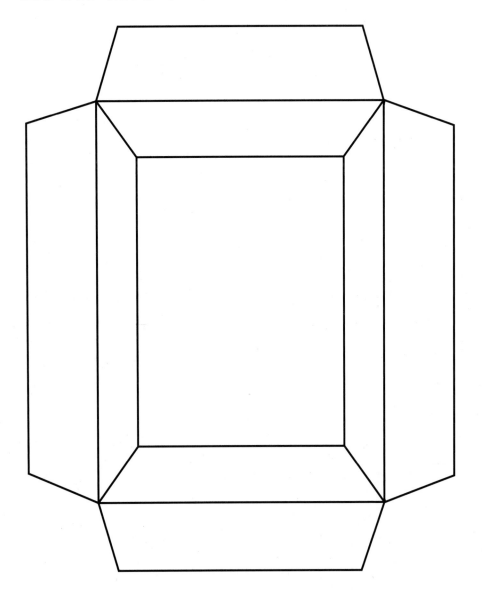

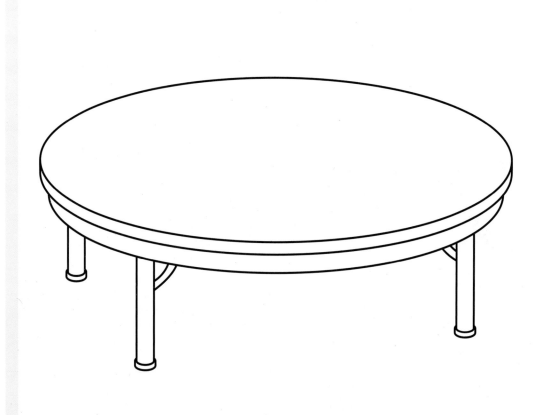

in the box

on the table

Count and trace.

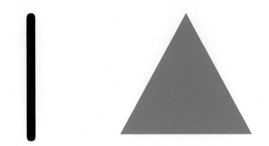 

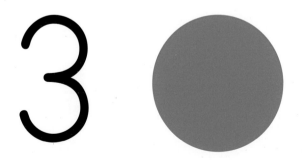 

Look and match. Color.

  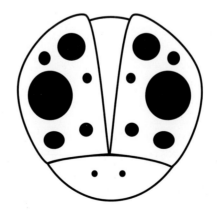 

Pre-reading Practice: Identifying and matching for visual discrimination

Look and listen. Trace.

Draw and Color

Are they listening to the teacher?
Look and color the correct face.

Values: We respect the teacher and listen.

Trace the numbers and follow the trails.

AMAZING

1

2

3

Amazing: Science Connection: *snail, trail*

MY SCHOOL

Draw your school.

2 MY SENSES

Find and circle.

FIND IT: *banana (taste), bee (hear), ball (touch)*

Draw the missing body parts. Color.

Vocabulary Practice: *eyes, hands, nose, ears, tongue*

Circle or cross out.

Vocabulary Practice: *see, hear, smell, taste, touch*

Match and color.

Vocabulary Review: *touch, hear, see, smell, taste*

Count and Color.

✂ **Cut out, match, and paste.**

Pre-reading Practice: Identifying and matching for visual discrimination
Phonics Practice: Initial Sound /s/

🎧 **4**

Look and listen. Draw the arrow to the next picture.

Guessing Game

Story Sequence: *Guessing Game*

UNIT 2
17

VALUES

Are they waiting for their turn?
Look and match.

Values: We are polite and wait for our turn.

Look and match.

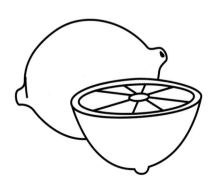   

MY SENSES

Draw something you can smell and something you can hear.

3 MY FAMILY

Find and circle.

Trace and color.

Vocabulary Practice: *grandmother, grandfather, aunt, uncle*

Point and say. Draw a cousin or a pet.

Trace and draw or paste photos of family members.

Vocabulary Review: Family members; *house*

Count and color. Write the missing numbers.

1 _ 3 4 _ 6 7 _ 9

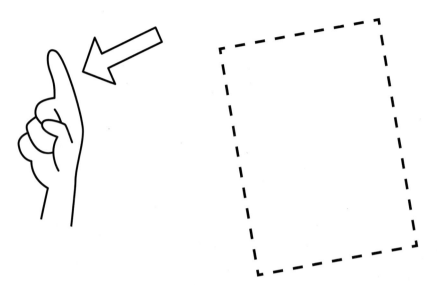

✂ Cut out, match, and paste.

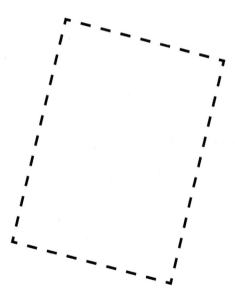

5 Look and listen. Draw an arrow to the next picture.

Show and Tell

Do they appreciate their family members?
Look and color the correct face.

Values: We appreciate family members.

Trace, draw more eggs, and color.

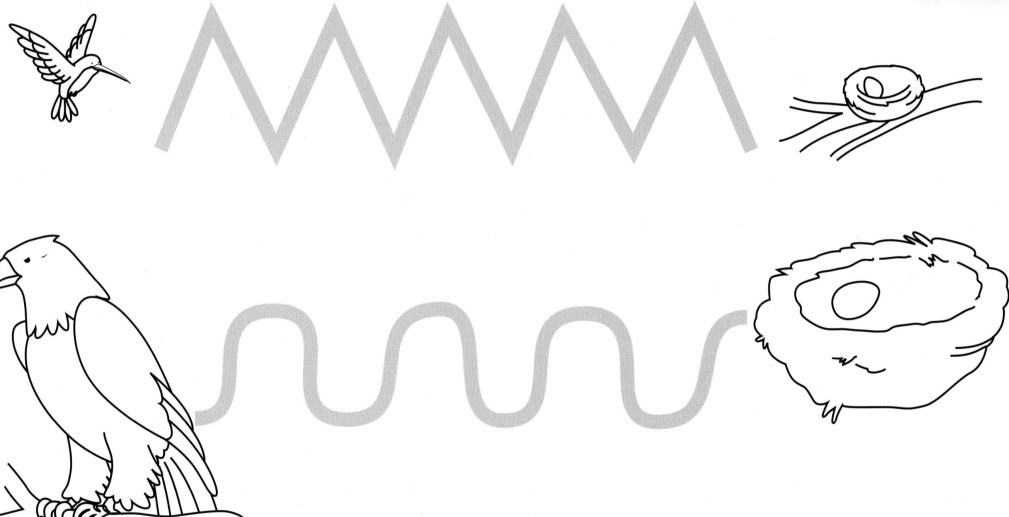

MY FAMILY

Draw your family.

4 MY TOYS

Find and circle.

Same or different? Color the frames if the pictures are the same.

Vocabulary Practice: *slide, swing, tricycle, car*

Circle a toy you have in blue. Then circle a toy you want in green.

I have 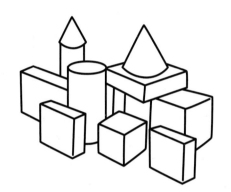 BLUE

I want GREEN

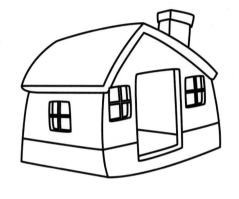

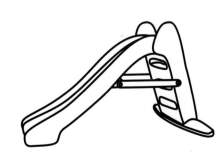

Vocabulary Practice: *blocks, action figure, play house, game, tricycle, slide*
Vocabulary Review: *doll, teddy bear*

Color the crayons. Then color by number.

Vocabulary Review: *car, teddy bear*; colors; numbers

Count, trace, and color.

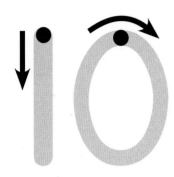

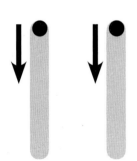

Draw an animal and say the sound.

Pre-reading Practice: Big and small animals help explain how letter names and sounds work.

Look and listen. Draw an arrow to the next picture.

Outdoor Fun

Are they sharing? Color the correct face.

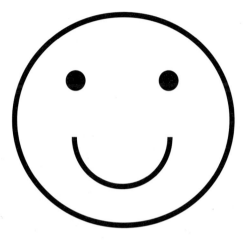

Values: We share to make something together.

Look. Circle or cross out.

I can see...

I can hear...

I can touch...

Amazing: Science Connection: *clouds, thunder, lightning, rain*

MY TOYS

Draw your toys.

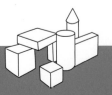

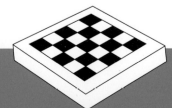

5 FOOD

Find and circle.

FIND IT: *carrot, cookie, apple*

Point and say. Draw food that you like.

Vocabulary Practice: *meat, fish, oranges, salad*

✂ Do you like…? Trace. Then cut out and paste.

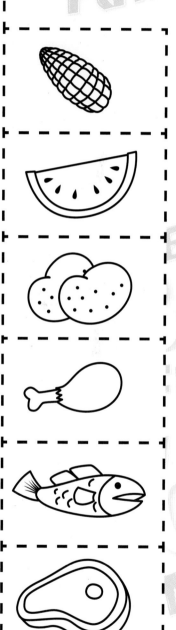

Vocabulary Practice: *corn, watermelon, potatoes, chicken, fish, meat*

What do you want to eat? Choose a food or a drink in each section and circle.

Vocabulary Review: *salad, soup, chicken, meat, fish, milk, juice, watermelon, cookies*

Count and trace.

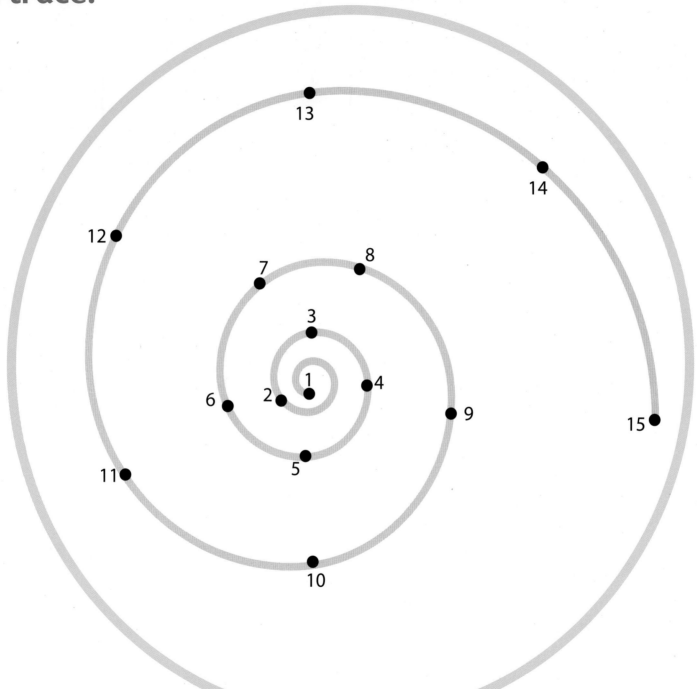

Trace. Circle the items that begin with /s/.

S S

S s

S s

S s 6

S s

S s

Pre-reading and Pre-writing Practice: *Ss*
Phonics Words: *sandwich, socks, soup, seal, six, sun*

I Like Apples

Are they using table manners?
Look, trace, and draw a happy or a sad face.

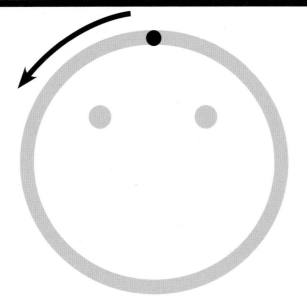
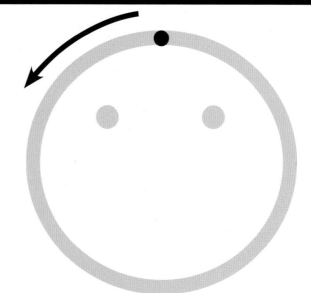

Values: We use table manners.

Color and paste orange tissue paper balls on the tree.

Amazing: Science Connection: *fruit, seeds*

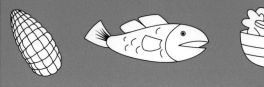

FOOD

Draw your favorite food.

6 MY CLOTHES

Find and circle.

Color the crayons. Then trace and color by number.

1 GREEN 2 PINK 3 ORANGE 4 YELLOW 5 BLACK

Vocabulary Practice: *shorts, sandals, hat, bathing suit*

✂ Cut out and paste the clothes.

Vocabulary Practice: *umbrella, raincoat, boots, jacket*

Look and draw the weather.

Vocabulary Practice: *rainy, sunny*
Vocabulary Review: *raincoat, umbrella, hat, boots, bathing suit, shorts, sandals*

Count and draw one more. Then trace and color.

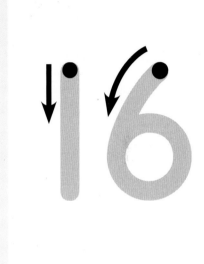

Trace and match with items that begin with /m/.

Pre-reading and Pre-writing Practice: *Mm*
Phonics Words: *monkey, meat, milk, moon, mouth, muffin*

Look and listen. Draw an arrow to the next picture.

How Many?

VALUES

Who is helping? Look and match.

Values: We help others.

Color and paste brightly colored paper feathers.

Amazing: Science Connection: *parrot, feathers*

MY CLOTHES

Draw your favorite clothes.

7 ANIMALS

Find and circle.

Match and color.

Vocabulary Practice: *rabbit, cow, sheep, chicken*

Draw a horse in the barn. Trace and color.

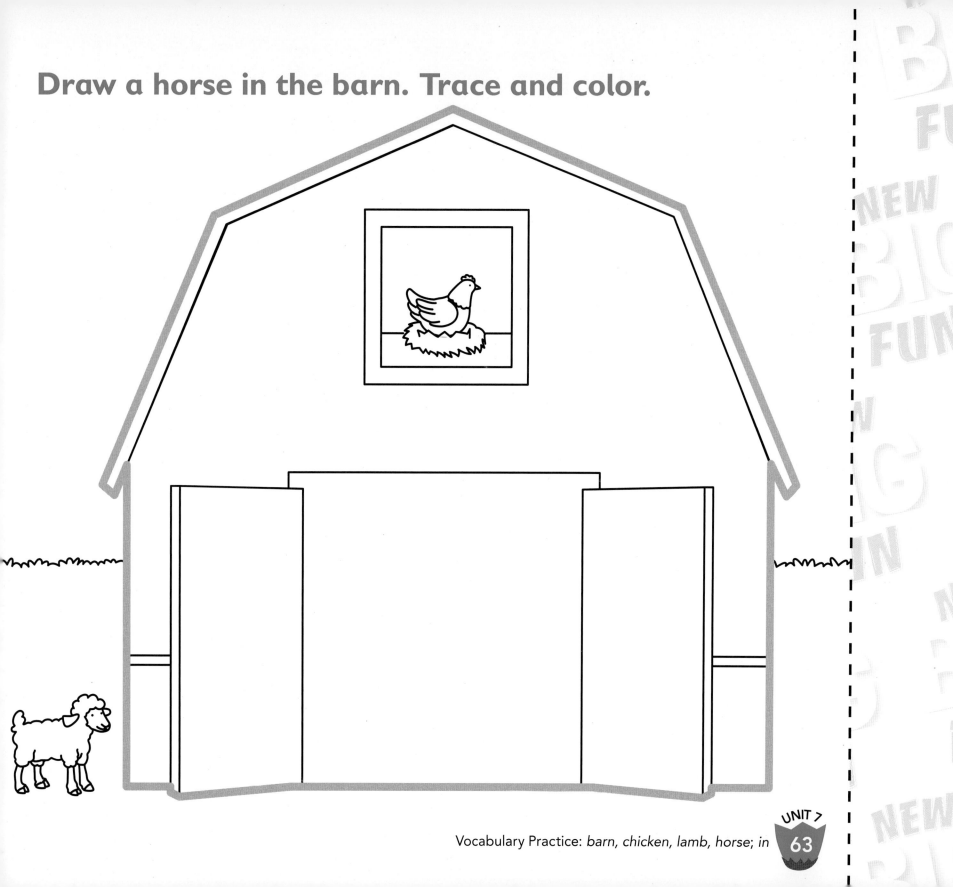

✂ **Cut out and paste two animals. Say.**

Vocabulary Review: *rabbit, chicken, cow, horse*
Language Practice: *This is a (rabbit). That is a (horse).*

Connect the dots and color. Draw your favorite pet.

Trace and write. Color things that begin with /l/.

Pre-reading and Pre-writing Practice: *Ll*
Phonics Words: *lemon, lion, lamb, leaves, lollipop, lemonade, lizard*

Look and listen. Draw an arrow to the next picture.

Where Are the Lambs?

VALUES

Are they taking care of the animals? Color the correct face.

Values: We take care of animals.

Number, trace, and draw a chick in the broken eggshell.

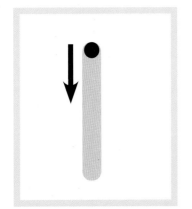

ANIMALS

Draw your favorite farm animals.

Find and circle.

Where are they? Look and match.

 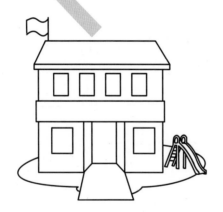 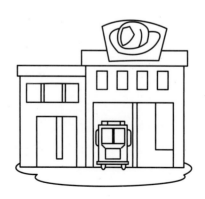 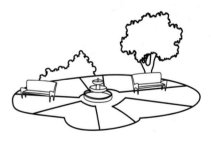

Vocabulary Practice: *restaurant, school, fire station, park*

✂ Cut out and paste the places. Say.

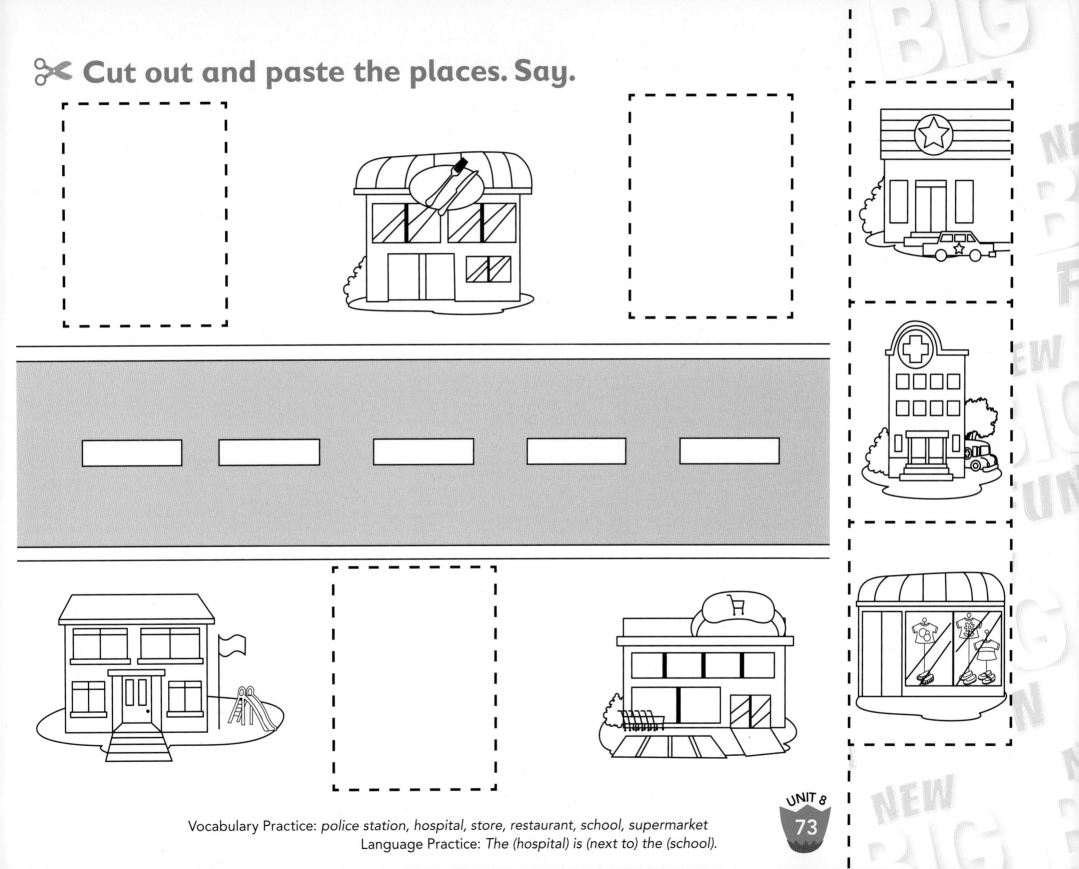

Vocabulary Practice: *police station, hospital, store, restaurant, school, supermarket*
Language Practice: *The (hospital) is (next to) the (school).*

Draw a person or pet in the window. Trace and color.

fire truck

Vocabulary Review: *fire truck, firefighter*

Count and color 20 fire trucks. Complete the number line.

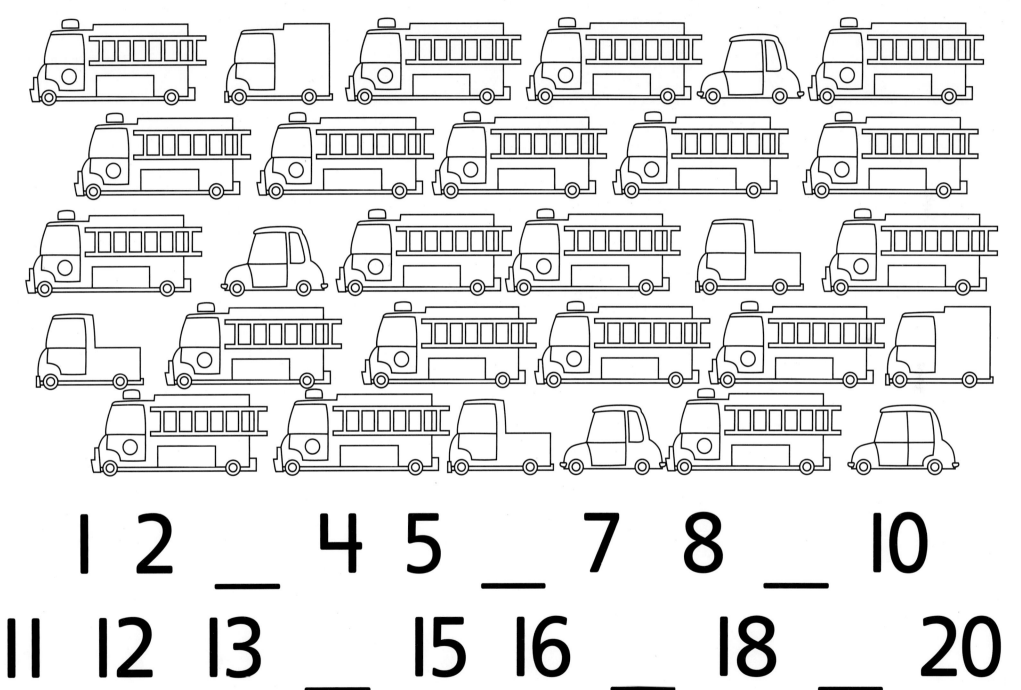

1 2 _ 4 5 _ 7 8 _ 10

11 12 13 _ 15 16 _ 18 _ 20

Trace. Circle the items that begin with /f/.

Pre-reading and Pre-writing Practice: *Ff*
Phonics Words: *fish, flower, five, farmer, feet, firefighter*

Shopping with Mommy

Look and match.

Trash

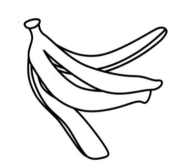

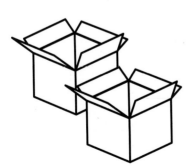

Trace the moons. Draw a moon in the sky and color.

Amazing: Science Connection: *crescent moon, half moon, full moon, telescope*

MY WORLD

Draw your favorite place.

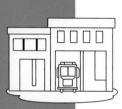
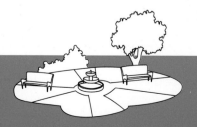

Look and review.

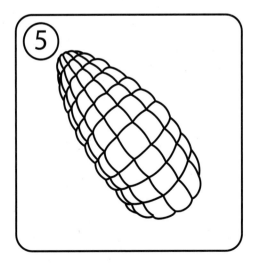

Review Units 1–8: *scissors, nose/smell, aunt/uncle/cousin, tricycle, corn, shorts, lamb/sheep, hospital*

Unit 1: Look and say. Color the objects you use inside a classroom.

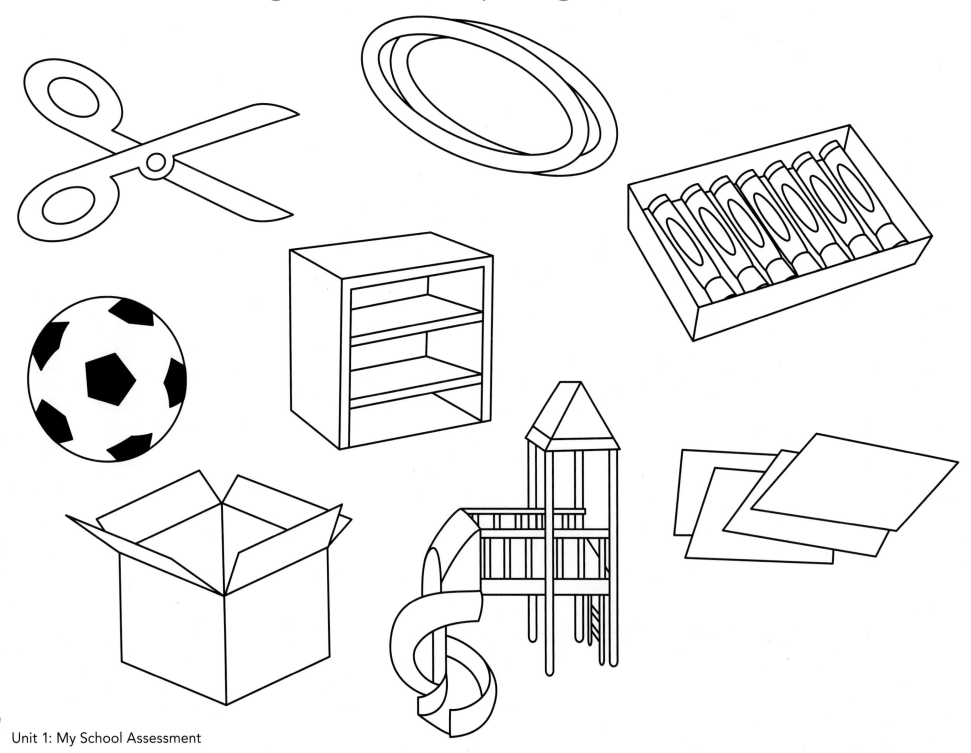

Unit 2: Look and match what you hear, smell, and taste.

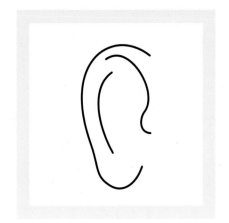
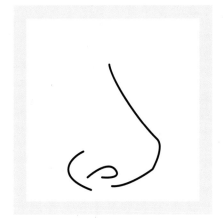
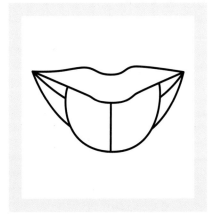

Unit 3: Name the family members and pets. Circle the type of home you live in.

Unit 4: What toys do you have? Look and circle.

UNIT 9

Unit 5: What do you like? Look and complete the faces.

Unit 6: What is missing? Look and match.

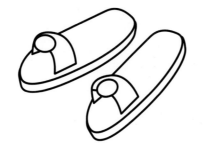

Unit 7: Where are the animals? Look and say.

Unit 7: Animals Assessment

Unit 8: Where is the…? Place a marker and say.

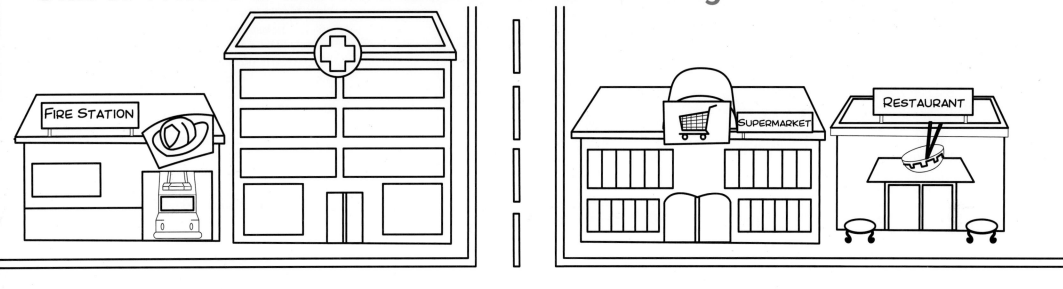

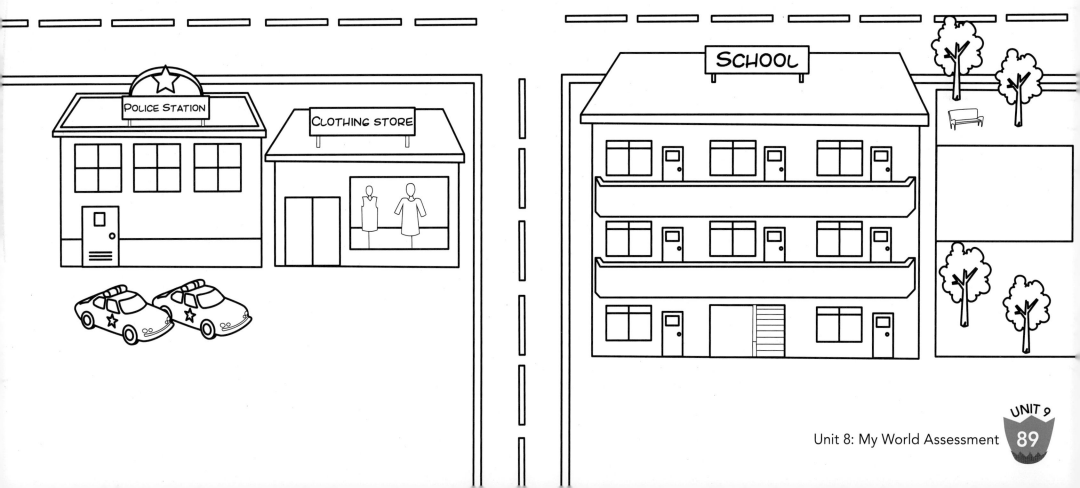

Workbook Audio CD

red yellow blue green

blue black

_____
has finished *New Big Fun* **Workbook 2!**

Good job!

pink white

orange purple brown pink